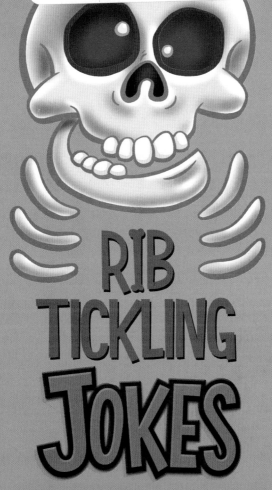

RIB TICKLING JOKES

Compiled by Emma van Dodeweerd

INDEX
BOOKS LTD

This edition published 2007 for Index Books Ltd.,
Garrard Way, Telford Way Industrial Estate,
Kettering, Northants, NN16 8TD
Copyright © 2005 Top That! Publishing plc
Tide Mill Way, Woodbridge, Suffolk, IP12 1AP, UK
All rights reserved
www.topthatpublishing.com
Printed and bound in China
0 2 4 6 8 9 7 5 3 1
Components sourced from Republic of China

What would
happen if you ate yeast
and polish?

You would rise and shine.

Doctor, Doctor, I get a terrible pain in
my eye whenever I drink milkshake.

Try taking the spoon out of the glass.

Doctor, Doctor, I don't feel well.

Try taking your gloves off.

What's yellow and swings
from one Christmas cake to another?

Tarzipan.

Where's Hadrian's Wall?

In front of Hadrian's house.

What musical instrument do Spanish fishermen play?

Cast-a-nets.

How do you make an apple puff?

Chase it round the garden.

Teacher: Johnny, when I was a child, I was told that if I made an ugly face, it would freeze and I would stay like that.

Johnny looked up and replied, Well, you can't say you weren't warned.

How many idiots does it take to change a light bulb?

Only one, but it takes eight years.

How many lawyers does it take to change a light bulb?

How many can you afford?

What do you get when you cross a pit bull terrier with a collie?

A dog that runs for help... after it bites your leg off.

Why does an elephant paint his feet yellow?

So he can't be seen hiding upside down in a bowl of custard.

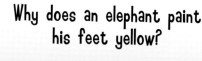

Why does an elephant paint his toenails red?

So he can't be seen hiding in a cherry tree.

What do you call a man with a seagull on his shoulder?

Cliff.

What do you call a man with a rabbit in his pocket?

Warren.

Doctor, Doctor, I keep thinking I'm a sack of mail.

Don't worry, we'll soon have you sorted.

Hey Dad,
I got A star for my essay on halogen light bulbs.

That's brilliant, son!

The doctor examines the patient on the couch and says, You seem all right to me, what was the problem?

I keep thinking I'm a television.

Turn over then, we'll see what's on the other side.

Knock knock.
Who's there?
Sonya.
Sonya who?
Sonya shoe I can smell it.

Bestseller - *Cats in the Bed* by Claude Bottom

A girl kept taking other people's passports. She took hundreds of them before the police caught up with her. They found a whole suitcase full of them under her bed. However, they let her off as it was a case of miss-taken identities.

What do you get if you cross an eagle with a skunk?

A bird that smells to high heaven.

Hungry cat to owner:

I want my dinner and I want it miaow.

What's the last thing to go through a mosquito's mind when it hits the windscreen?

Its bum.

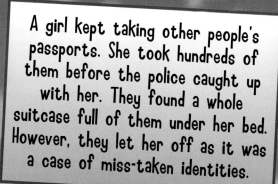

What do you call a gorilla
with a machine gun?

Sir.

Why do
elephants have
wrinkles?

Because they don't
like ironing.

Knock knock.
Who's there?
Mandy.
Mandy who?
Man de lifeboats, we're sinking.

Doctor, Doctor, I keep thinking I'm
a traffic warden.

What do your friends say?

Friends, what friends?

What do you call a mobile phone with a flat battery?

A dead ringer.

Then there was the Irish dentist called Phil McCavity!

Two boys were walking along the street when one found a pay packet on the pavement. He opened it, took out the £5 and stuffed it in his pocket. He was just reading the details on the payslip when the other boy said, Its all right for you, you have all the luck. Luck, he said, look at the tax they stopped me.

One cow says to the other, It's a bit worrying, this mad cows disease.

Doesn't affect me, said the other, I'm a horse.

Doctor, Doctor, I keep thinking I'm a pair of curtains.

Don't be stupid and pull yourself together.

Knock knock.
Who's there?
Emma.
Emma who?
Emma fed up of waiting for you to open the door.

Did you hear about the sea scout who went camping?

His tent sank.

Doctor, Doctor, I keep imagining I'm a locked wardrobe.

I'll send you to a psychiatrist, maybe you'll open up to him.

Teacher, on opening end-of-year present from little Johnny,
Thank you Johnny, that's very kind of you, but why have you given me a snail?

Because I couldn't get a snake.

The meek shall inherit the earth - if that's all right with everybody else.

How do you stop a rooster crowing on Sunday?

Eat him on Saturday!

Why did the foal cough?

Because he was a little horse!

Why did the pig go
to the casino?

To play the slop machine!

What
looks like half a cat?

The other half!

What happened when the
cat ate a ball of wool?

She had mittens!

What did the cat say when
he lost all his money?

I'm paw!

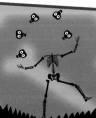

How do you know if your cat has eaten a duckling?

She's got that down in the mouth look!

What is the cat's favourite TV show?

The evening mews!

What noise does a cat make going down the highway?

Miaoooooooooooooooooooooooooooooooow!

Why did the cat join the Red Cross?

Because she wanted to be a first-aid kit!

What's the definition of a
nervous breakdown?

A chameleon on a tartan rug!

What do
headmasters and bullfrogs
have in common?

Both have big heads that consist
mostly of mouth!

What happened when a frog
joined the cricket team?

He bowled long hops!

What did the bus conductor
say to the frog?

Hop on!

When is
a car like a frog?

When it's being toad!

Why do bears have fur coats?

Because they'd look stupid in anoraks!

What animal do you look like
when you get into the bath?

A little bear!

How do you hire a teddy bear?

Put him on stilts!

What did the lion say to his cubs when he taught them to hunt?

Don't go over the road till you see the zebra crossing.

What does a lion brush his mane with?

A catacomb!

What happened when the lion ate the comedian?

He felt funny!

Why is a sofa like a roast chicken?

Because they're both full of stuffing!

Why did
the chicken cross the
road, roll in the mud and
cross the road again?

Because he was a dirty
double-crosser.

Why didn't the chicken skeleton
cross the road?

Because he didn't have enough guts.

Why did the dinosaur cross the road?

Because chickens hadn't evolved yet.

Why didn't
the two worms get on
Noah's Ark in an apple?

Because everyone had to
go on in pairs!

How can you tell
which end of a worm is which?

Tickle it in the middle and see
which end laughs!

Why was the glow-worm unhappy?

Because her children weren't that bright!

What did
the woodworm say to the chair?

It's been nice gnawing you!

What's yellow, wiggles and is dangerous?

A maggot with attitude!

What do
you get if you cross a
glow-worm with a python?

A foot strip light that can
strangle you to death!

What is a worm's favourite band?

Puddle of Mudd!

What do you call a flea
that lives in an idiot's ear?

A space invader!

What is the difference
between a flea and a wolf?

One prowls on the hairy and the
other howls on the prairie!

How do you find where
a flea has bitten you?

Start from scratch!

What did
the idiot do to the
flea in his ear?

Shot it!

What is the difference between
school dinners and a pile of slugs?

School dinners come on a plate!

What did the slug say as
he slipped down the wall?

How slime flies!

Where do you find giant snails?

At the end of giants' fingers!

How do you know if you have a tough mosquito?

You slap him and he slaps you back!

What's the difference between a lawyer and a mosquito?

A mosquito drops off you when you die!

Why are mosquitos religious?

They prey on you!

What happened when the cannibals ate a comedian?

They had a feast of fun!

What happened at the cannibal's wedding party?

They toasted the bride and groom!

How can you help a starving cannibal?

Give him a hand!

What was the cannibal called who ate his father's sister?

An aunt-eater!

What happens
if you upset a
cannibal?

You get into
hot water!

What does a cannibal call
a skateboarder?

Meals on wheels!

What did the cannibal say when he
came home and found his wife chopping
up a python and a pygmy?

Oh no, not snake and pygmy pie again!

What's the definition of a
cannibal?

Someone who goes into a restaurant and
orders a waiter!

What did
the cannibal say
when he was full?

I couldn't eat
another mortal!

What did the cannibal
make of her new friend?

A hotpot!

Why did the cannibal have a hangover?

He went to a party and got stewed!

Why didn't the
skeleton go to the party?

He had no body to go with!

What happened when the skeletons rode pogo sticks?

They had a rattling good time!

How did the skeleton know it was going to rain?

He could feel it in his bones!

What do you call a skeleton who won't get up in the mornings?

Lazy bones!

What do you call a dog owned by Dracula?

A blood hound!

What was the Californian
vampire hippy like?

He was ghoul man, real ghoul!

What happened
to the mad vampire?

He went a little batty!

Why did the
vampire take up acting?

It was in his blood.

What do eskimos sing at parties?

Freeze a jolly good fellow...!

Man: Doctor, Doctor. My wife thinks she's a clock!

Doctor: Well, stop winding her up then!

Why are fruit trees such cry-babies?

People are always picking on them!

Young Boy: Can I buy some bird seed, please?

Pet Shop Owner: How many birds have you got?

Young Boy: None, I want to grow some!

Teacher: The bell's gone, Gary.

Gary: I didn't take it!

Why are clocks dirty?

Because they work hours a day, and never wash their hands or face!

What would happen if everyone in the country bought a pink car?

We would have a pink carnation.

A man who worked in the butcher shop was 6 feet tall, had red hair and wore size 10 shoes. What did he weigh?

Meat.

What wobbles when it flies?

A Jelly-Copter!

What did the big chimney
say to the little chimney?

You're too young to smoke!

Why did the skeleton cross the road?

To get to the Body Shop!

How do you stop an
elephant from charging?

Take away its credit cards!

What do you give a sick canary?

Tweetment!

What happens
when two snails have a fight?

They slug it out!

How do you make your coat last?

Make your trousers first!

Why do golf players wear two
pairs of trousers?

In case they get a hole in one!

Why was
six afraid of seven?

Because seven
eight nine!

How does a penguin build his home?
Igloos it together!

Why did Santa lose his job?
The elves gave him the sack!

How do you join the police force?
Handcuff them all together!

Why was the hammer sorry?
Because it hit the nail on the head.

Why did the burglar
take a shower?

He wanted to make a
clean getaway.

What do you get if you
cross an elephant with a kangaroo?

Big holes all over Australia.

Doctor, Doctor,
I feel like a car.

Just park there. I'll be with
you in a minute.

Doctor, Doctor. Can you
give me anything for my wind?

Certainly, here's a kite.

How many ears has Captain Kirk?

Three. The left ear, the right ear, and the Final Frontier!

What do you call a boomerang that doesn't work?

A stick.

Why are there so many Smiths in the phone book?

They all have phones.

Nurse: Doctor, there's a ghost in your waiting room.

Doctor: Tell him I can't see him.

Why did the orange stop rolling down the hill?

Because it ran out of juice.

Doctor, Doctor, I've only got seconds to live!

I'll be there in a minute!

Where do sheep get their hair cut?

The baa baas.

What did Santa say to his wife on Christmas Eve?

Do not go out in the reindeer.

Waiter, waiter, have you got frogs legs?

No sir, this is the way I have always walked.

What did the stupid ghost do?

He climbed over walls!

A man walked into a pet shop. Have you got any puppies going cheap? he asked.

No sir, the pet-shop owner replied. All our puppies go yap, yap.

Our budgies go cheap!

Two men walked into a bar, what did they say?

Ouch!

What did the biscuit say when he was run over by a lorry?

Oh, crumbs!

Why is a river so rich?

Because it flows between two banks.

Why did the man throw his clock out of the window?

To make time fly.

Why did the girl swallow her £5 note?

Because her mother said that it was for her lunch!

What did the baby-corn ask its mum?

Where's pop-corn?

Why did
the hedgehog cross the road?

To see his flat mate!

What did the fish say
when he swam into a wall?

Dam!

Two crisps were walking down the road when a taxi pulled up. Do you want a ride? said the driver.

No thanks, we're Walkers! they replied.

Why did the sparrow
fly into the library?

It was looking for
bookworms!

Two cows were standing in a field.
One said mooooooo.

The other said I was about to say that!

What do you call a deer with no eyes?

No eye deer!

Why were
there police cars and
ambulances gathered round the chippy?

A fish had been battered!

What is
a witch's favourite lesson?

Spelling.

What do you call a greedy crab?

Shellfish!

Doctor, Doctor, I feel
like a pack of cards!

I'll deal with you later.

Doctor, Doctor,
I think I'm a moth.

So why did you come around then?

Well, I saw this light at the window...!

Doctor, Doctor, I've broken my arm in two places.

Well, don't go back there again then!

Mum, can I have a dog for Christmas?

No, you can have turkey like everyone else!

Knock Knock.
Who's there?
Mary.
Mary who?
Mary Christmas!

Do you know the time?

No, we haven't met yet!

Waiter, this soup tastes funny?

Then why aren't you laughing!

What has a bottom at the top?

I don't know?

Your legs!

Mr Smith: I hate to tell you, but your wife just fell down the wishing well.

Mr Brown: It works!

Why did the idiot have his sundial floodlit?

So he could tell the time at night!

How do you keep an idiot
happy all his life?

Tell him a joke when he's a baby!

What do
you call a dog that
makes a bolt for the door?

Blacksmith!

What do you call a man with
a pile of soil on his head?

Doug!

What do you call a pig with an itch?

Pork scratching!

What do you call
a deaf monster?

Whatever you like –
he can't hear you!

What do
you call a man with a
karaoke machine?

Mike!

What do you call a
sheep that says Moo?

Bilingual!

What do you get if you
cross a pig with a naked person?

Streaky bacon!

What do you get if you cross a road with a safari park?

Double yellow lions!

What do you get if you cross a box of matches and a giant?

The big match!

What do you get if you cross a kangaroo with a skyscraper?

A high jumper!

What do you get if you cross a cow with a grass cutter?

A lawn mooer!

What do you get if you cross
an ice cream with a dog?

Frost-bite!

What do you get if you cross
a helicopter with a Cornish pasty?

Pie in the sky!

What do you get if you
cross a Viking and a detective?

Inspector Norse!

What do you get if you cross a
large computer and a beefburger?

A big mac!

What do you get if you cross an overheating large computer with a beefburger?

A big mac and fries!

What do you get if you cross a naked woman and the bottom of the ocean?

A deep sea Lady Godiva!

What do you call a man who forgets to put his underpants on?

Nicholas!

What do you call a man who wears tissue paper trousers?

Russell!

How does Posh Spice keep
her husband under control?

He's at her Beckham call!

What do
you call a mummy that
washes up?

Pharaoh Liquid!

What do you call a man
who cleans out toilets?

Lou!

What do you call a woman
that people sit on?

Cher!

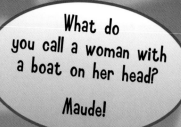

What do you call a woman with a boat on her head?

Maude!

What do you call a woman who throws her bills on the fire?

Bernadette!

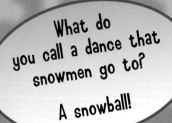

What do you call a dance that snowmen go to?

A snowball!

What do you call two elephants at the swimming pool?

A pair of swimming trunks!

What runs around your garden all day and never stops?

The fence!

What do you call a fish that can't swim?

Dead!

What do you call a bull you can put in the washing machine?

Washable!

Is this a second-hand shop?

Yes, sir.

Good. Can you fit one to my watch then please!

What kind of
cat lives in the sea?

An octopuss!

Why did
the cowboy die with his
boots on?

Because he didn't want to stub
his toe when he kicked
the bucket!

What did the fireman's
wife get for Christmas?

A ladder in her stocking!

I don't
think these photographs
you've taken do me justice.

You don't want justice - you
want mercy!

How do you stop a cold getting to your chest?

Tie a knot in your neck!

What steps would you take if a madman came rushing at you with a knife?

Great big ones!

How do you cure a headache?

Put your head through a window and the pane will just disappear!

I was once in a play called 'Breakfast in Bed'.

Did you have a big role?

No, just toast and marmalade!

What lies at the bottom
of the sea and shivers?

A nervous wreck!

What did the tie say to the hat?
You go on ahead and I'll hang around!

What did
the picture say
to the wall?

I've got you
covered!

I want a hair cut please.

Certainly, which one!

Who broke
the window?

It was Bob, he ducked
when I threw a stone
at him!

You were a long time putting salt
in the salt cellar.

Well, you can't get much at a time
through those little holes at the top!

Why was the Egyptian girl worried?

Because her daddy was a mummy!

It's
time for your
violin lesson.

Oh, fiddle!

How old is your granddad?

I don't know but we've had him a long time!

Dad, there is a man at the door collecting for the new swimming pool.

Give him a glass of water!

Eat up your spinach, it'll put colour in your cheeks.

But I don't want green cheeks!

Quick, take the wheel, said the nervous driver.

Why?

Because there is a tree coming straight for us!

Why did Mickey Mouse
take a trip into space?

He wanted to find Pluto!

What happened when
the wheel was invented?

It caused a revolution!

Did you hear about the mad scientist
who put dynamite in his fridge?

They say it blew his cool!

Why didn't the banana snore?

Because it didn't want to wake
up the rest of the bunch!

Did you hear about the little boy that they named after his father?

They called him Dad!

Did you hear about the stupid tap dancer?

He fell in the sink!

How did the witch know she was getting better?

Because the doctor let her get out of bed for a spell!

Why is it easy to swindle a sheep?

Because it is so easy to pull the wool over its eyes!

What is
the only true
cure for dandruff?

Baldness!

What should you buy if your hair falls out?

A good vacuum cleaner!

What do you call a cowboy
who helps out in a school?

The deputy head!

What position
did the witch play in
the football team?

Sweeper!

What position did the pile of wood play in the football team?

De-fence!

Why couldn't the slow boxer get a drink at the party?

Because everyone beat him to the punch!

Why was the archaeologist upset?

His job was in ruins!

Why was the butcher worried?

His job was at steak!

Why did
the teacher have to
turn the lights on?

Because his pupils were
so dim!

Why did the French farmer
only keep one chicken?

Because in France one egg is un oeuf!

What do you call a man
who can lift a car?

Jack.

Why is the sand wet?

Because the seaweed.

Why did the class eat all their homework?

The teacher said it was a piece of cake.

What kind of egg can you throw?

A chuckie egg.

What do you call a cow eating grass?

A lawnmooer.

What's the quickest way to count a herd of cows?

Use a cowculator.

The idiot who locked himself out of his car tried to open it by forcing a wire coat hanger through to pull the handle. Meanwhile the other idiot inside the car said, left a bit, down a bit!

How does a rhinoceros climb a tree?

He sits on a seed and waits.

Why did the boy throw a clock out of the window?

He wanted to see time fly.

What kind of beans do sharks like?

Human beans.

What's a lion's favourite christmas carol?

Jungle bells.

Why didn't Cupid shoot his arrow at the traffic warden's heart?

Because even Cupid can't hit a target that small!

What did one oar say to the other?

Can I interest you in a little row-mance?

What does a carpet salesman give his wife for Valentine's Day?

Rugs and kisses!

What is your favourite type of present?

Another present!

How does Moby Dick celebrate his birthday?

He has a whale of a party!

When's your birthday?

April 20th.

What year?

Every year!

What did one candle say to the other?

Don't birthdays burn you out?

Why couldn't prehistoric man send birthday cards?

The stamps kept falling off the rocks!

I guess I didn't get my birthday wish.

How do you know?

You're still here!

Doctor, I get heartburn every time I eat birthday cake.

Next time, take off the candles.

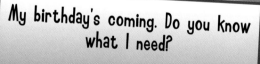

My birthday's coming. Do you know what I need?

Yeah, but how do you wrap a life?

Why won't anyone eat the dog's birthday cake?

Because he always slobbers out the candles!

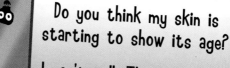

Do you think my skin is starting to show its age?

I can't tell. There are too many wrinkles.

How can you tell if an elephant's been to your birthday party?

Look for his footprints in the ice cream.

Were any famous people born on your birthday?

No, only little babies.

For his birthday the monster asked for a heavy sweater.

So they gave him a sumo wrestler!

While visiting a farm, some children saw a farmer with a big load of manure.

What are you going to do with the manure? one of the children asked.

I'm going to spread it on the strawberries, replied the farmer.

Haven't you tried sugar and cream?

The little boy picked up an adder by its tail and swung it round and round.

Look what I found Mum, a tail without a dog!

Why do cows wear bells around their necks?

Because their horns don't work.

How did you find the weather on holiday?

It was easy. I just left the hotel - and there it was!

Idiot: My friend here keeps thinking he's invisible.

Which friend's that?

Johnny: I beat my friends up every morning.

Susie: Really?

Johnny: Yes. I'm up at seven o'clock. They all sleep until eight!

Johnny: This is a good place for a picnic.

Susie: How do you know?

Johnny: All these flies can't be wrong!

Why did your sister cut a hole in her new umbrella?

Because she wanted to be able to tell when it stopped raining.

Did you hear about the idiot who wrote himself a letter and forgot to sign it and when it arrived he didn't know who it was from?

Johnny: I was so mad I could have punched Arthur in the nose!

Susie: Well, what stopped you?

Johnny: Arthur!

Why did the idiot wear a wet shirt all day?

Because the label said, 'Wash and Wear'.

Then there was the girl who spent two weeks in a revolving door looking for the doorknob.

Johnny: What happened to you?

Susie: I fell while I was riding.

Johnny: Horseback?

Susie: I don't know. I'll go and check the stable.

Johnny: Why are you putting the saddle on backwards?

Susie: How do you know which way I'm going?

Did you put the cat out?

Why, is it on fire?

Johnny: Why did your sister feed money to her cow?

Susie: Because she wanted to get rich milk.

Old man: My wife finds it very difficult to eat these days.

Friend: Why's that?

Old man: She never stops talking.

Why did you tiptoe past the medicine cabinet?

Because I didn't want to wake the sleeping pills.

Did you hear about the woman who went on a crash diet?

She looks a wreck!

Then there was the girl who fell in love at second sight.

When she first met him she didn't know how rich he was.

Why did the idiot jump up and down before taking medicine?

Because the label said Shake well before using.

What do you do if your nose goes on strike?

Picket!

A man recently ran out of the supermarket with a trolley load of prunes without paying. He has so far been on the run for three days.

How do you get a baby
astronaut to sleep?

You rock-et.

Johnny: My dog has no nose.

Susie: How does he smell?

Johnny: Absolutely awful.

Did you hear about the cat that
ate coins and bank notes?

There was always money in the kitty.

Said the e-spider
to the e-fly: Be sure to
visit my website.

What do you get if you cross a rambler with a parrot?

A walkie talkie.

Why did the elephant paint her head yellow?

To see if blondes have more fun.

Doctor, Doctor, my friend thinks he's a motorcycle.

Get him to take these pills and he'll be fine.

Then who's going to give me a lift to work?

What do you call a skeleton that won't do any work?

Bone idle.

What's the difference
between teachers and
chocolate?

Kids like chocolate.

Johnny: My sister is a real swot.

Susie: I bet she gets high marks in her exams.

Johnny: No, but she kills lots of flies.

What do you call a
French sandal salesman?

Phillippe Flop.

What has eight legs, eats
grass and is very expensive?

Two deer.

What do you call a horse who goes around the world?

A globetrotter.

Where does the congregation sit in the Church of England?

In the British Aisles.

First library assistant: I see Mr. Smith has returned all his books at last.

Second library assistant: There must be at least 100 in that box - and for some reason a pair of trousers

First library assistant: There's a turn up for the books.

What do you call a man who clears drains?

Rod.

Why was the tyrannosaurus rex always panicking?

Because he was prehysterical.

How do you stop an elephant stampede?

Make a trunk call and reverse the charge.

Johnny and Susie went to the shop and Johnny bought some sweets. On the way home he noticed that Susie was carrying some eggs.

I didn't see you pay for those, he said.

I didn't need to, it said they were free-range eggs!

Did you hear about the turkey who escaped from the farm six times until he was sold for Christmas?

He was foiled in the end.

What did the red toilet say to white toilet?

I'm feeling rather flushed today.

A man was arrested just as he was about to throw a woman, with her feet set in concrete, in the river.

He explained that it was his mother-in-law and he wanted to cement the relationship.

Johnny: Does the beach end when you go in the sea?

Susie: Probably, but can't be shore.

What did the policeman say when he found three deep holes in the ground?

Well, well, well, what 'ave we 'ere?

What do bread rolls do
at the weekend?

They normally just loaf around.

What do you call a ram
who eats natural foods.

An organic butter.

100 people all said they
preferred fresh food to tinned food.

The coincidence was uncanny.

There was a huge flood in
Amsterdam. When the men went down
into the city's sewers to investigate,
they found they were all clogged up!

What do you call a multi-talented Welsh poet?

Dai Verse.

What song do they sing at the Lumberjack of the Year Awards?

For he's a jolly good feller!

Green match to red match: Is that your girlfriend?

Red match to green match: No, just an old flame.

Susie: Why do you have that big poster of a baseball player in your room?

Johnny: It's my favourite pitcher.

What do you call a man
with a two-way radio?

Roger.

What do you get if you
put banana skins in the oven?

Warm slippers.

Johnny: I sent my big sister's photo
to a dating agency.

Susie: That's terrible, and you'll get into trouble.

Johnny: It's OK, they sent it back, said they
weren't that desperate!

Young lady: Doctor, I've got these
terrible pains in my stomach.

Doctor: OK let's have a look then.
Mmmm. You've got acute appendicitis.

Young lady: Don't be cheeky, just tell me
what's wrong with me.

What do you get if you put eyeballs in the freezer?

An icy stare.

In what country are you not allowed to wear an open-necked shirt?

Thailand.

Olga and Rudolf were lying in bed one night on their little Russian farm.

Sounds like squirrels on the roof again, said Olga.

No, its raining, replied Rudolf.

How can you tell?

Rudolf the Red knows rain, dear!

Johnny: I think our teacher's great.

Susie: I prefer reading, I can shut the book up!

What do you get if you cross a poker player with a dash to the toilet?

A running flush.

Which sea creature tells dirty jokes?

A blue whale.

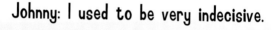

Johnny: I used to be very indecisive.

Susie: So what's new?

Johnny: Now I'm not so sure.

What do you get if you cross a sheep and a frog?

A woolly jumper.

Policeman: What's afoot here then?

Boy: Same as usual, officer, about 12 inches.

Hey, isn't that a bacon tree?

Careful, looks like an 'ambush!

What's the difference between a buffalo and a bison?

You can't wash your hands in a buffalo.

Doctor, Doctor, I keep thinking I'm a pear.

Do you both feel this way?

Is your face hurting you?

No, why?

Because it's killing me!

Knock, knock.

Who's there?

Teresa.

Teresa who?

Trees are green of course.

What's the difference
between an anorak and a coat?

A coat doesn't go trainspotting.

What happens when scouts start
rowing with each other at camp?

You get an intents argument.

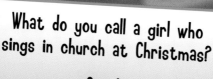

What do you call a girl who sings in church at Christmas?

Carol.

Johnny: My feet are killing me.

Susie: What have you been doing?

Johnny: Climbing mountains in Scotland

Susie: You must have Cairncorns.

What's the difference between a bowl and a dish?

You can't get satellite TV with a bowl.

There were two Canadian hunters. The one at the rear said, Get a move on, I've got a bear behind.

Well, pull your trousers up and you'll be able to run faster!

In which country are
ice machines made?

Cuba.

My wife's gone to
the Caribbean.

Jamaica?

No, she decided herself.

I've decided to go to
the Far East for a while.

Korea?

No, for a holiday.

Which country has special
paths for rodents?

Gnaw way.

In which country are you
most likely to catch a cold?

Qatar.

What did one phone say
to the other?

You're too young to be engaged.

What do
you call a man who writes
out invoices?

Bill.

What do
ghosts wear when
it's wet?

A ca-ghoul.

What is
the most common type of
book in the prehistoric world?

A thesaurus!

Who are the most patient
people in the world?

Kuwaitis.

In which country doesn't
it pay to be a pop star?

Singer poor.

What do
you call a man bouncing up
and down in a swimming pool?

Bob.

What do you call a man who grades examination papers?

Mark.

What do you call an actor who wins lots of awards?

Oscar.

What do you call a man who carries a bayonet?

Spike.

What do you call a man who thinks he's a haystack?

Rick.

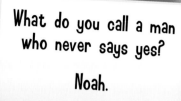

What do you call a man who never says yes?

Noah.

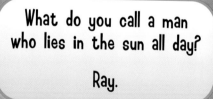

What do you call a woman who tests DNA samples?

Jean.

What do you call a man who lies in the sun all day?

Ray.

What do you call a man who lives down a dark passage?

Ali.

What do
you call a man who
collects carts
and carriages?

Orson.

What do you call a man caught
with a bag of stolen goods?

Robin.

What do you call a man who is good at DIY?

Andy.

What do
you call a woman
whose body is spreading?

Marge.

What do you call a woman who grows flowers?

Rose.

What do you call a man with no hair?

Shaun.

What do you call a man who grows rice?

Paddy.

What do you call a man who sells compost?

Pete.

What do you call a man who loves having a bonfire?

Bernie.

What do you call a woman who does police car impersonations?

Nina.

What do you call a cricketer when he isn't run out?

Justin.

What do you call a girl who lives on the beach?

Sandie.

What do
you call a man who likes
English country dancing?

Maurice.

What do
you call a woman who
is always being sick?

Eva.

What do you call a man
who is a fitness fanatic?

Jim.

What do you call a man
who's always saying prayers?

Neil.

What do you call a woman who is always gambling?

Bet.

Where is England's biggest cemetery?

Bury.

Where is England's biggest coal fire?

Stoke.

Where are the best swimmers in England?

Poole.

Where are
the best card
players in England?

Deal.

Where do all the women panic so
much they get their knickers in a twist?

Nottingham.

Where in London can you
never find the children?

Hyde Park.

Where are the cleanest beaches in England?

The Wash.

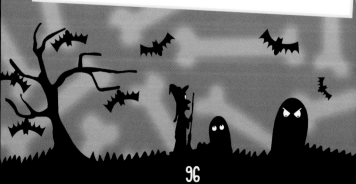

Dentist: I'm afraid your tooth
needs to come out.

Patient: Are you sure? Is that
the tooth, the whole tooth
and nothing but the tooth?

What do you call a man
who operates a crane?

Derrick.

What do you get if you cross a
nudist with food, water and air?

Bare essentials.

What do
you get if you cross
a road with an old lady?

Appreciation.

What do you get if you plant a row of beans stretching a mile?

Long-distance runners.

What do you call a man who everybody walks all over?

Matt.

Which kind of tree gets homesick?

The pine tree.

What do you call a man who has had his motor stolen?

Carlos.

What do
you call a man who
has lots of debts?

Owen.

What do you call a woman who
says prayers before every meal?

Grace.

What do you call a girl who
never stops babbling?

Brooke.

What do you call a girl
who is always angry?

Maddy.

What do you call a girl who works at the crab factory?

Shelley.

What do you call a girl who likes big churches?

Abbie.

What do you call a man who can do anything?

Abel.

What do you call a girl who catches butterflies?

Annette.

Which trees do bears climb?

Fur trees.

What do you call a woman
who goes to lots of auctions?

Biddy.

What
do you call a girl
who gets up very
early in the morning?

Dawn.

What do you call a man who
gets a job as a cleaner?

Dustin.

What do you call a man who lives in a Scottish valley?

Glen.

What do you call a woman who is absolutely nuts?

Hazel.

What do you call a woman who is mad about boats?

Marina.

What do you call a man carrying meat, potatoes and carrots?

Stewart.

Bestseller: *The Agony of Acne* by Lance Boil

Bestseller: *Climbing Trees* by Ivy Dussit

Bestseller: *Irritation* by Ivan Awfulitch

Bestseller: Knickers round your ankles by Lucy Lastic

What did the hunter
say to the waiter?

Get me a crocodile sandwich
and make it snappy!

How do you make someone burn their ear?

Ring them up when they're ironing.

Where would
you fly a flag in
space?

On the Pole Star.

Which shellfish won the Marine
Weightlifting Contest?

Mussels.

What kind of fish would you see through the windows of the space shuttle?

Star Fish.

What do you get if you cross a builder with a chicken?

A brick layer.

What kind of fruit do you find in a horse's stable?

Strawberries.

The lion, the tiger and the leopard all pulled out of the Big Cats World Poker Competition because none of them wanted to play a cheetah.

What kind of musical instrument costs £1,000?

A grand piano.

Which insects live on polar bears?

Arc-tics.

What kind of tree do you always find by the sea?

A beach tree.

Camel to waiter: A cup of coffee please.

Waiter: Sugar?

Camel: Yes please.

Waiter: One lump or two?

An elephant dropped a pile of dung in the middle of the motorway.

Police advised motorists to treat it as a roundabout.

What do you call a man who spins round and round?

Eddy.

Why did the blacksmith throw a party for the whole village?

He wanted to forge new friendships.

Where is the centre of the Scottish candle-making industry?

Wick.

How do you stop a bull charging?

Take away his credit card.

Cannibal to son: I've told you before not to mess about with the prisoners.

Son: Why not? It's good fun.

Cannibal: It's bad manners to play with your food.

Waiter to cannibal at a dinner dance: Shall I bring you the menu, sir?

Cannibal: No thanks, just the guest list.

Johnny: I got A star for my project on nuclear radiation.

Susie: That's excellent. I bet your parents are pleased.

Johnny: Yes, I got a glowing report.

What do Italians eat with their afternoon tea?

A pizza cake.

How do you tell the time in an Indian restaurant?

Just look at the chicken tikka.

The supermarkets brought out a new range of intelligent bread, but no one ever bought it. They all wanted thick sliced loaves.

What do you get if you put a cow in a spin drier?

Milk shake.

What do you get if you cross fish with a black and white keyboard?

A piano tuna.

What drink never stops complaining?

Whine.

What do you call a frog who goes to France for the day?

A Channel hopper.

What's green and turns red at the flick of a switch?

A frog in a liquidiser.

What sort of snake will tell on you?

A grass snake!

Where did the rich cat live?

In a mews cottage!

Boy in pet shop: How much are those squid?

Pet shop owner: Ten quid, sonny.

Boy: Ten quid? It looks a bit poorly.

Owner: Call it sick squid then!

Why did the farmer feed his pigs sugar and vinegar?

He wanted sweet and sour pork!

What sort of music
was invented by fish?

Sole music!

What gets
smaller the more you put in it?

A hole in the ground!

Is that a new perfume I smell?

It is, and you do!

What did the stupid burglar
do when he saw a 'WANTED' poster
outside the police station?

He applied for the job!

Why was the broom late?

It over swept!

How did the farmer fix his jeans?

With a cabbage patch.

Do you have any invisible ink?

Certainly sir. What colour?

What do you mean by telling everyone that I'm an idiot?

Sorry, I didn't know it was a secret!

This match won't light!

That's strange, it did this morning!

Why do cricketers have poorly stomachs?

Because they're always getting the runs.

What do you get when you cross a battery and a mummy?

A mummy who's in charge.

Johnny: This morning my mum gave me soap flakes instead of corn flakes.

Susie: I bet you were mad.

Johnny: Mad, I was foaming at the mouth!

Doctor:
You've got chickenpox. Its
lucky you spotted it early.

Where would you find all
the world's breeds of cattle?

In a mooseum.

Optician:
You need new glasses.

Patient: How can you tell without
an eye test?

Optician: I could tell the moment
you walked through
the window.

Doctor, Doctor, I think I'm a bridge.

What on earth's come over you?

Ten cars, three motorbikes and a bus.

Dog: Where do fleas go in winter?

Cat: Search me.

Doctor, Doctor, I think I've got a split personality.

You'd better both sit down.

Doctor, Doctor, how long can you live without a brain?

That depends. How old are you now?

Doctor, Doctor, I keep bumping into things.

You need glasses.

Will I be able to read with them?

Yes.

That's good because I didn't know how to before.

What did Adam say on the day before Christmas?

It's Christmas, Eve!

A woman was given a canary for her fortieth birthday so she called it 40.

The canary died a couple of years later so she got another one and called it 40 too.

What do you call a penguin in the Sahara desert?

Lost!

What's white, furry and smells minty?

A polo bear!

What's the difference between an iceberg and a clothes brush?

One crushes boats and the other brushes coats!

What do reindeer say before telling you a joke?

This one will sleigh you!

What's the best way to speak to a monster?

From a long way away!

How do you make a racehorse fast?

Don't feed it!

How long
should a dog's legs be?

Just long enough to reach
the ground!

Why did the zebra wear
sunglasses on the beach?

Because he didn't want to be recognised!

Which goats have the shortest legs?

The smallest ones!

Where do you find ponies?

It depends on where you leave them!

How is a strawberry
like an apple?

They're both green,
except the strawberry!

On which
side of the house did
Jack's beanstalk grow?

The outside.

What did Snow White say when
the shop lost her photographs?

Someday my prints will come.

Why did Robin Hood steal from the rich?

Because there was nothing to take
from the poor.

What did
the idiot call his
pet zebra?

Spot.

How can you get a set of
teeth put in for free?

Thump a lion!

What does the eagle say to his friends
before they go out hunting for food?

Let us prey.

What happens
when a lion runs into an
express train at the station?

It's the end of the lion!

What do you call a woodpecker with no beak?

A headbanger.

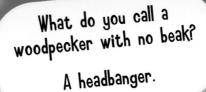

When is the best time to buy budgies?

When they're going cheap!

Which bird is always out of breath?

A puffin.

What's got six legs and can fly long distances?

Three swallows.

What is a polygon?

A dead parrot.

How do you know that owls are much cleverer than chickens?

Have you ever heard of Kentucky-fried owl?

What did the salad bowl say to the cucumber, the tomato, the onion and the beetroot?

Lettuce all be friends.

Where do sheep go to drink?

To a baa.

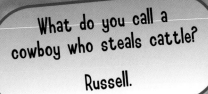

What do you call a
cowboy who steals cattle?

Russell.

What do you call a man
who holds tents down?

Guy.

What do you call a man
who thinks he's a cat?

Tom.

What do you call a
woman who grows herbs?

Rosemary.

What do you call Rosemary's husband who also grows herbs?

Basil.

What do you call a girl when she gets to the end of a long march?

April.

What's the difference between a hectare and an acre?

You wouldn't call a dog Acre.

What's the difference between art and skill?

Have you ever heard of a skill transplant?

Did you hear about the cricketer whose dinghy was sinking?

He thought he was going to drown until he bailed himself out.

What's the difference between a tree and a locked up dog?

One sheds its bark, the other barks in a shed.

Why did the mouse catcher eat cheese?

So he could watch his traps with bated breath.

Man lost in desert: How far is it to the sea?

Nomad: About 200 miles.

Man: In that case I'll stay on the beach.

Why did the head teacher
ban school uniforms?

Because the blazers were
a fire hazard.

What's the difference
between a border and a boundary?

A boundary doesn't pay rent.

What is black, sweet,
prickly and goes for long walks?

A brambler.

What do you get if you cross a
broom with a policeman?

A brush with the law.

Doctor, Doctor,
I keep thinking I'm a hen.

Just lay over here,
will you?

Doctor, Doctor, I keep
thinking I'm a politician.

Now come on, tell the truth.

What's the difference
between a boy and a girl?

A girl doesn't always float.

Bestseller: *To Hell and Back*
by Gladys Allover

Bestseller:
How to be a Good Neighbour
by Linda Hand

Bestseller: *Make Yourself Heard*
by Meg Aphone

Bestseller: *Rude Answers*
by Kurt Response

Bestseller: Greek Food
by Donna Kebab

Why was Granny Smith so fond of the Golden Delicious?

Because she was the apple of her eye.

What's the difference between a satsuma and a mandarin?

Satsumas never ruled China.

What did the orange sing to the clementine?

Oh my darlin', oh my darlin', oh my darlin' clementine.

What do prisoners use to call each other?

Cell phones.

What kind of fruit do bees like?

Nectarines.

What do you get if you cross
Victoria with the Greek alphabet?

Plum Pi.

What fruit
does a footballer eat
when he's sent off?

Man go.

What's a cat's favourite fruit?

Paw Paw.

What fruit did the boy give his girlfriend for Valentine's Day?

Passion fruit.

What's the difference between two calves and two heifers?

You'd never get two heifers in a pair of trousers.

Why is it sad to eat cauliflowers and melons?

Because it makes you melancholy.

Why is a broken ankle bone the quickest to recover from?

Because it's always the next to heel.

What do you get if you cross some plums with lots of cars?

Traffic jam.

What's the difference between your back and your belly?

Depends how fat you are!

What did the politicians say when the Health Minister announced better services for the deaf?

Ear ear.

Johnny: How would you describe the smell of chocolate?

Susie: I've no idea.

Johnny: Go on just try.

Susie: It's... well it's like... oh Heaven nose!

What's the
difference between your
hips and your waist?

You can recycle waste.

Doctor, Doctor, I keep
thinking I'm an envelope.

We must stamp this out right away.

Johnny: What's the difference
between a doctor and a dentist?

Susie: I don't know.

Johnny: Well I 'd keep my mouth
shut if I were you.

What's the difference between
a traffic warden and a cream bun?

Cream buns are nice.

How much are policemen paid?

Only coppers.

Did you hear about the footballer that used perfume?

He was scent off!

Son of headmaster: My dad's four times better than your dad.

Son of army officer: No he's not, mine's better than yours.

Son of headmaster: What does your dad do then?

Son of army officer: He's a quartermaster.

What does Father Christmas say when he's gardening?

Hoe Hoe Hoe.

What's the
difference between a
burglar and a politician?

You can trust
a burglar.

What's the difference between a
liver and a kidney?

Kidneypool hasn't got a football club.

What's the difference between
a club and a society?

You can't play golf with a society.

What's worse than finding a
maggot in your apple?

Finding half a maggot.

Budgie: Where are you going for your holidays?

Parrot: I think I'll go to the Canaries.

Where would you find a crab that makes speeches?

The Seychelles.

Where would you find the Andes?

On the end of the armies.

Two climbers are on the way up Everest when they see a cockerel.

Climber: Brilliant, we'll have fresh eggs for breakfast.

Climber: Don't be stupid, only hens lay eggs.

Climber: He's different, Himalaya!

One cockerel to another: Are you married then?

No, divorced. In fact there goes my eggs wife now.

Johnny: Did you know that all marine creatures play football?

Susie: Don't be stupid, how can they?

Johnny: Well there are 20,000 leagues under the sea.

Why did the idiot take a pencil to bed?

To draw the curtains.

Why don't feet need to go to school?

Because they have their own trainers.

What's the difference between knickers and pants?

Have you ever heard of a dog that knickers?

There's a new mint flavoured after shave just come out.

Its best worn with a polo neck.

Headmaster: So you admit it then Johnny. It is very naughty to flick paper pellets at Teacher's bottom.

Johnny: Yes sir. I'm sorry sir.

Headmaster: I've decided not to give you the cane this time but for your punishment you will suck this lemon.

Johnny: Suck a lemon sir?

Headmaster: Yes, it'll wipe the smile off your face.

What type of fruit grows on your body?

A navel orange.

What type of vegetable doesn't hold water?

A leek.

Careers Officer: Have you any ambitions, Johnny?

Johnny: Yes, I've always wanted to be a travel agent.

Careers Officer: I can see you'll go far.

Why would a demolition expert make a good comedian?

Because he's guaranteed to bring the house down.

Teacher: Where is the English Channel?

Pupil: I don't know, my TV doesn't pick it up.

Two necks and a head ran the 100 metres. They all went over the line roughly together.

I was a head, said the head.

No you weren't, it was neck and neck, said the teacher.

A woman was very conscious about being fat, but one day she found a lamp and rubbed it. The genie came out and granted her one wish.

I really want to lose all my unsightly fat.

The genie granted the wish and the woman's head disappeared.

Teacher: What can you tell me about the Dead Sea?

Pupil: Dead? I didn't even know it was ill!

What's the best place to buy a present for a cat?

In a cat-alogue.

Doctor, Doctor, I keep thinking I'm a packet of fish fingers.

Gimme five!

What do you get if you cross a Dutch mug with an Italian cravat?

A European Cup tie.

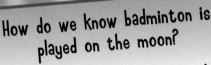

How do we know badminton is played on the moon?

Why else would we have a space shuttle?

What do you get if you cross the English theatre with an Australian kangaroo?

An international show jumper.

Doctor, Doctor,
I've swallowed my watch.

Don't worry, time passes
very quickly.

Did you hear about the boy who
had a soft spot for his teacher?

It was quicksand.

Bestseller: *No More Toothache*
by Freda Pain

Bestseller:
Indecision by Willy Orwontee

Doctor, Doctor, I keep
thinking I'm a teapot.

You pour thing.

What do big cats read
in the newspaper?

Head-lions!

Did you hear about the idiot who had
such a bad itch he went to the
newsagent and bought a scratch card?

Where would
you find a white horse, a
black horse and an Arab horse?

At a race meeting.